Mesopotamia

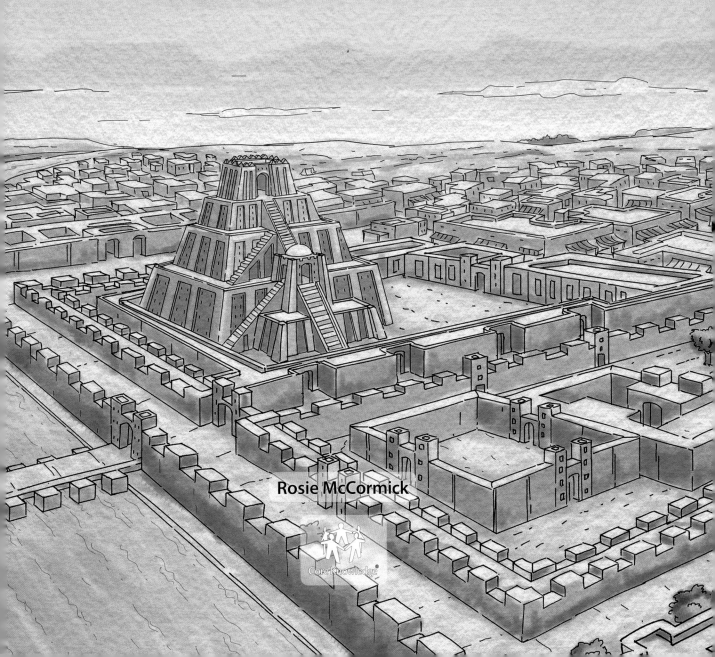

Rosie McCormick

CoreKnowledge®

ISBN: 978-1-68380-388-1

Mesopotamia

Table of Contents

Ancient Times

Long, long ago, people moved from place to place gathering plants and hunting animals for food. Sometimes they lived in simple huts.

Over time, people learned to farm. They grew plants that could be eaten as food. Slowly, groups of people began to live together.

The ancient Mesopotamians became so good at farming that some people had time to do other things. They built cities that had buildings, streets, and gardens. Mesopotamian kings and queens lived in these beautiful cities, along with other people. The Mesopotamians created a great civilization.

The Land Between Two Rivers

The name Mesopotamia means "between the rivers." The land of Mesopotamia lay between the Tigris and Euphrates Rivers. Because there was water nearby, the land was good for farming. Farmers grew the food that fed the people of Mesopotamia, including those who lived in the cities.

The kings of Mesopotamia were in charge of the cities. Their job was to protect the cities, the people, and the farmland from enemies.

Many of the cities in Mesopotamia were built with walls around them for protection. This is what a walled city would have looked like long ago.

People had many different kinds of jobs in the cities of Mesopotamia. Some people, called craftsmen, made pots, baskets, clothes, and jewelry. Others carried people by boat from place to place.

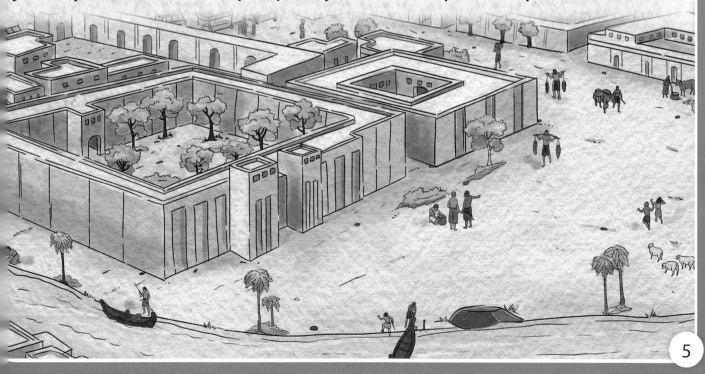

The farmers grew food in the fields outside the city walls. The Tigris and Euphrates Rivers were important. Sometimes the rivers flooded. The floodwater carried rich soil into the fields that was good for growing plants. At other times, when there wasn't enough rain for the plants, river water was brought to the fields.

City Life in Ancient Mesopotamia

Some people in Mesopotamia knew how to read and write. They didn't write on paper. Instead they used reeds to make marks on wet clay. This way of writing is called cuneiform. Having a way to write down important information helped make the Mesopotamian civilization great.

Kings were powerful leaders. They led armies into battle. They made peace too. This piece of art made from shells and stones shows people bringing special gifts to the king.

Children in Mesopotamia played with toys, just like children do today. What do you think this is?

Queens were important too! They helped to make decisions. A queen in Mesopotamia once wore this gold headdress and jewelry. The headdress was made to look like the leaves of a tree.

King Hammurabi's Written Laws

Hammurabi was a great king in Mesopotamia.

He created the Code of Hammurabi. This was a set of laws that were written down so that everyone would know them. Writing down important information and ideas is one way a civilization can be strong.

King Hammurabi wanted all Mesopotamians to follow the laws. People knew if they broke a law, they would be punished. This is a statue of Hammurabi kneeling down.

Gods, Goddesses, and Temples

In ancient Mesopotamia, people believed in many gods and goddesses. Temples were places where people went to pray to the gods and goddesses.

They also asked the gods and goddesses to help them. This is a statue of a person asking a god for help. You see, people believed that the gods and goddesses could make good and bad things happen.

Because the gods and goddesses were thought to be so powerful, people built great temples to them.

This is a photograph of the ruins of the Temple of Ur. Thousands of people would have gone to this temple. It still stands today in the modern-day country of Iraq.

The Mesopotamians built temples to honor their gods, but they also built other things. Babylon was the richest city in Mesopotamia. This beautiful gate in the city of Babylon was built to honor Ishtar, the goddess of love and war.

People in Mesopotamia told stories about how strong and brave one of their kings was. His name was King Gilgamesh. They also showed his bravery in pictures.

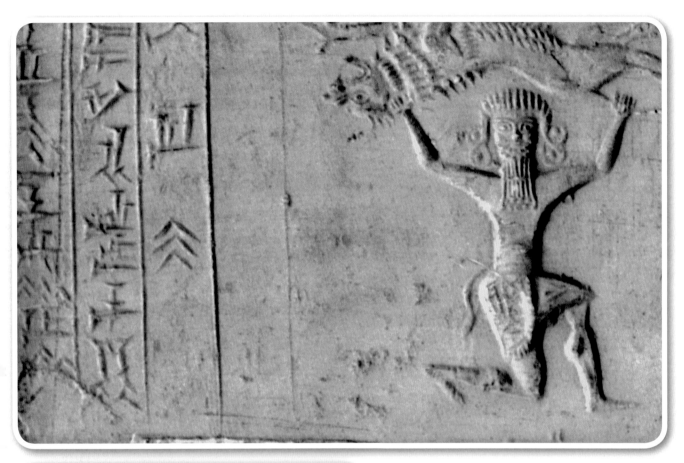

The stories and pictures tell that King Gilgamesh was so strong that he could defeat a lion. King Gilgamesh did so many amazing things; he was thought to be a half-god.

Core Knowledge®

CKHG™

Core Knowledge HISTORY AND GEOGRAPHY™

Editorial Directors

Linda Bevilacqua and Rosie McCormick

Subject Matter Expert

Nadine Brundrett, Department of Classics, Brock University

Illustration and Photo Credits